6/13

Jellyfish

by **Trudi Strain Trueit**

Reading Consultant: Nanci R. Vargus, Ed.D.

Marshall Cavendish
Benchmark
New York

Picture Words

 arms

 bell

 jellyfish

 jellyfish

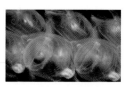 lights

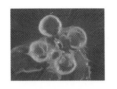 rings

 spots

 stripes

 tentacles

Look at the !

This has .

This  has |||||||.

This has .

This 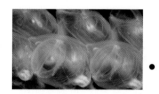 has 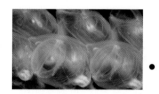 .

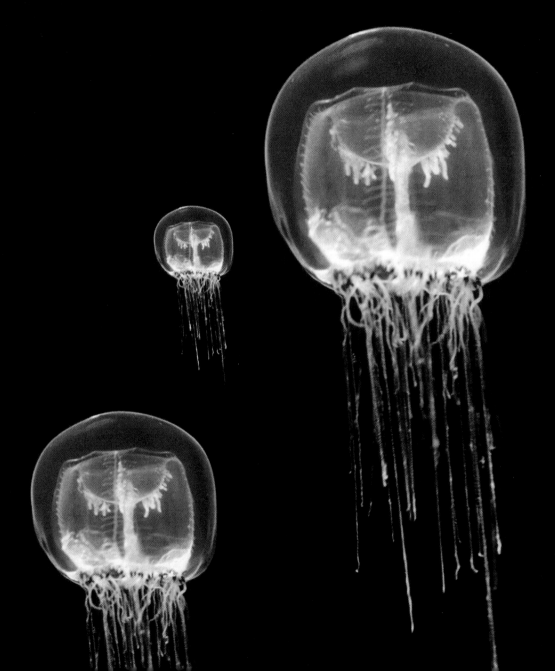

This has .

14

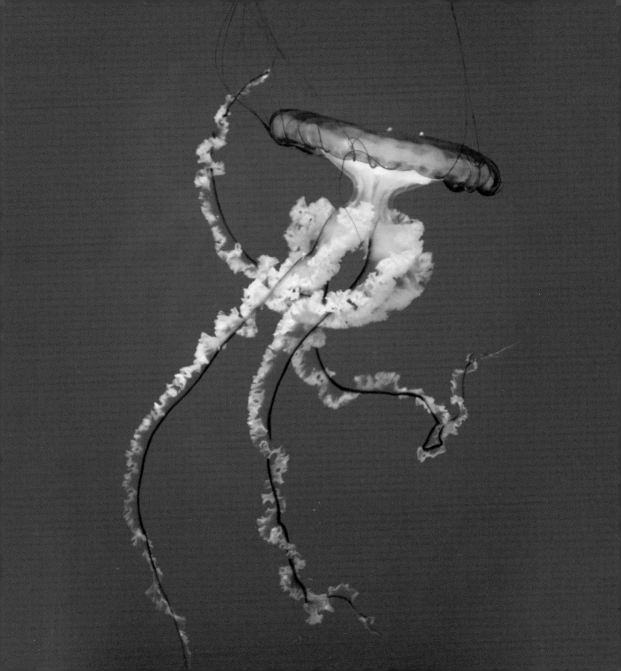

This  has a big .

This has .

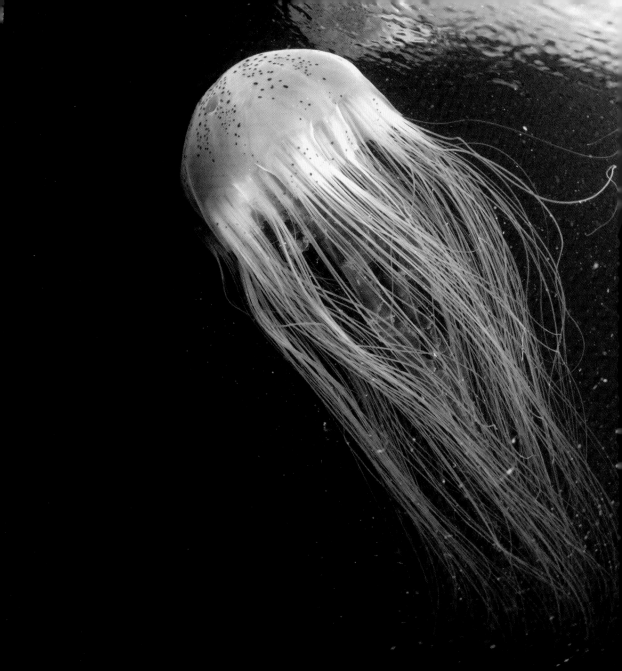

Look, but do not touch! sting.

Words to Know

jellyfish (JEL-ee-fish)
    a sea animal whose body feels like jelly

sting (STING)
    to hurt by pricking with a poison

tentacles (TEN-tuh-kuhls)
    the long, thin parts of a jellyfish used for feeling

Find Out More

Books

Herriges, Ann. *Jellyfish*. Minneapolis, MN: Bellwether Media, 2007.

Lunis, Natalie. *Gooey Jellyfish*. New York: Bearport, 2008.

McFee, Shane. *Jellyfish*. New York: PowerKids Press, 2008.

DVDs

Imax Deep Sea, Warner Home Video, 2006.

Ocean Life, PBS Kids, Lancit Media, 2008.

Websites

Monterey Bay Aquarium
www.mbayaq.org

Oceanic Research Group
www.oceanicresearch.org/education/wonders/lesson.html

Save Our Seas for Kids
www.saveourseas.com/minisites/kids/82.html

About the Author

Trudi Strain Trueit lives in Everett, WA, near Puget Sound, home to some of the world's largest jellyfish. The Lion's Mane jellyfish is her favorite. Trudi is the author of more than sixty fiction and nonfiction books for children, including *Octopuses* and *Sea Turtles* in the Benchmark Rebus Ocean Life series. She writes fiction, too, including the popular *Secrets of a Lab Rat* series. Visit her website at **www.truditrueit.com**.

About the Reading Consultant

Nanci R. Vargus, Ed.D., wants all children to enjoy reading. She used to teach first grade. Now she works at the University of Indianapolis. Nanci helps young people become teachers. She snorkeled near the jellyfish in the Great Barrier Reef, but she didn't touch them!

Copyright © 2011 Marshall Cavendish Corporation

Published by Marshall Cavendish Benchmark
An imprint of Marshall Cavendish Corporation

Website: www.marshallcavendish.us

This publication represents the opinions and views of the author based on Trudi Strain Trueit's personal experience, knowledge, and research. The information in this book serves as a general guide only. The author and publisher have used their best efforts in preparing this book and disclaim liability rising directly and indirectly from the use and application of this book.

Other Marshall Cavendish Offices:
Marshall Cavendish International (Asia) Private Limited, 1 New Industrial Road, Singapore 536196 • Marshall Cavendish International (Thailand) Co Ltd. 253 Asoke, 12th Flr, Sukhumvit 21 Road, Klongtoey Nua, Wattana, Bangkok 10110, Thailand • Marshall Cavendish (Malaysia) Sdn Bhd, Times Subang, Lot 46, Subang Hi-Tech Industrial Park, Batu Tiga, 40000 Shah Alam, Selangor Darul Ehsan, Malaysia

Marshall Cavendish is a trademark of Times Publishing Limited

All websites were available and accurate when this book was sent to press.

Library of Congress Cataloging-in-Publication Data
Trueit, Trudi Strain.
Jellyfish / Trudi Strain Trueit.
        p. cm. — (Benchmark rebus. Ocean life)
Includes bibliographical references.
Summary: "A simple introduction to jellyfish using rebuses"—Provided by publisher.
ISBN 978-0-7614-4891-4
1. Jellyfishes—Juvenile literature. 2. Rebuses—Juvenile literature. I. Title.
QL377.S4T78 2010
593.5'3—dc22
2009025934

Editor: Christina Gardeski
Publisher: Michelle Bisson
Art Director: Anahid Hamparian
Series Designer: Virginia Pope

Photo research by Connie Gardner
Cover photo by Chris Newbert/*Minden Pictures*

The photographs in this book are used by permission and through the courtesy of: *Getty Images*: p. 2 Frederic Parcorel, lights; p. 5 Steve Grundy; p. 21 Joe Drivas. *Art Life Images*: p. 7 age fotostock; p. 13 age fotostock; p. 19 age footstock. *Peter Arnold*: p. 9 Cole Brandon. *Minden Pictures*: p. 2 Hans Leijnse, bell; p. 3 Marc Spencer, stripes; Scott Leslie, tentacles; Fred Bravendoam, rings; pp. 11, 17 Fred Bravendam; p. 15 Kevin Schafer. *Corbis*: p. 2 Dani Cardona, arms, jellyfish; p. 3 Norbert Wu, spots.

Printed in Malaysia (T)
1   3   5   6   4   2